LET'S FIND OUT ABOUT

Telephones

LET'S FIND OUT ABOUT

Telephones

BY DAVID C. KNIGHT

Pictures by Don Miller

FRANKLIN WATTS, INC.
575 Lexington Avenue
New York, N. Y. 10022

SBN 531–00048–6

Copyright © 1967 by Franklin Watts, Inc.

Library of Congress Catalog Card Number: AC67-10006

Printed in the United States of America

by The Moffa Press, Inc.

6

LET'S FIND OUT ABOUT

Telephones

Sometimes two people want to talk to each
    other, but they are not close to each other.
What can they do about it?
They can use a telephone.

Telephones carry people's voices back and
   forth over a wire.
The people can be far apart in different
   cities.

Or they can be just a couple of rooms away.

You see people talking over telephones every
day.
What they are doing is telephoning, called
phoning.
Your father phones other men at the office.
Your mother phones other ladies at home.
You can learn to phone, too.
You can phone a friend.

Most of the time telephones are just called "phones."
When you phone someone you *make a call*.
Every phone has a special number of its own.
You can find the number by looking it up in a *telephone directory*.
Or by asking the *operator* for it.

Maybe your friend has already told you his
   number.
When you phone him, you usually
   dial his number.

But on some new phones you can push
buttons to get his number.

Telephones didn't always look the way they do today.

Thirty years ago phones looked like this:

75 years ago

Forty years ago phones looked like this:

Eighty years ago phones looked like this:

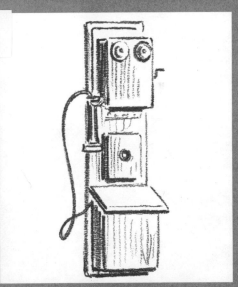

One hundred years ago there were no
phones at all.

17

When there weren't any telephones, how
    could a person in one city talk to somebody
    in another city?
He couldn't.
He would have to go to the other city.
Or he would have to write a letter.

Long ago, before people had phones, there
weren't any radios or airplanes, either.
Getting letters and messages back and forth
took days.
If a letter went by ship, it could take weeks
or even months.

Men began searching for other ways to send
messages over long distances.
One of them named Samuel Morse found a
way.
He invented the telegraph.
The telegraph could send messages between
cities by electricity over a wire.

Baltimore   *Washington, D. C.*

Electricity can travel very fast over a wire.
It can travel almost 186,000 miles in a single
  second!
But there was one big trouble with
  electrical telegraph messages.

They could only be sent in code — dots and
   dashes.
Only trained men could send them or read
   them.

So men began looking for an even better
way to send messages over a wire.
They began looking for a way to send a
voice over a wire.
One man finally did find a way.
His name was Alexander Graham Bell.

In 1876 –
136 years ago !!!

Alexander Graham Bell invented the first
   telephone.
He invented it almost one hundred years ago.
Bell's telephone did not look like our phones
   at all.
It was a funny looking thing.
But it worked!

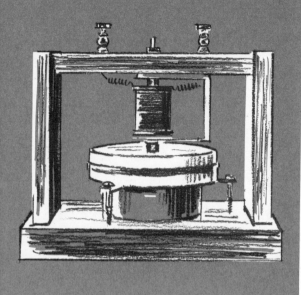

Bell's First Telephone

Bell's Second Telephone

*Bell's
Third Telephone*

Pretty soon a lot of people were using
   Mr. Bell's telephones.
In those days, hearing a voice coming out of
   a wire seemed like magic.
People could not figure out how this new
   thing called "the telephone" worked.

Today there are still many people who don't
know how telephones work.
They can't understand them.

How about you? Do you know how phones
   work?
Let's try to find out.

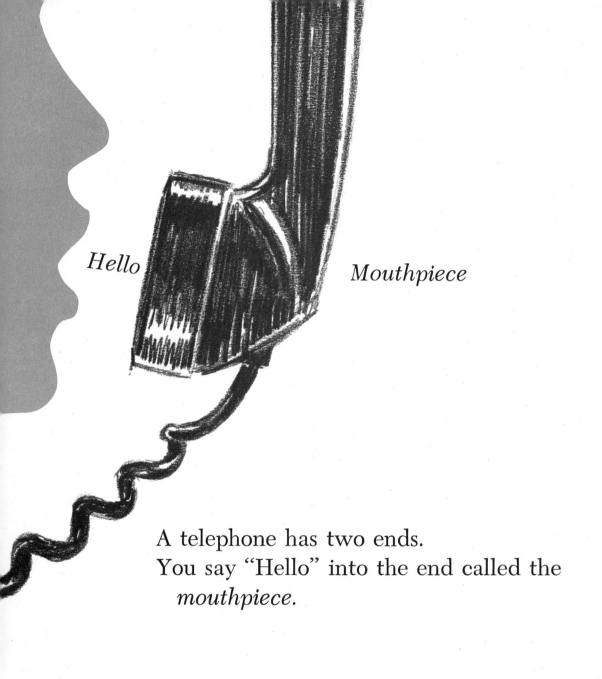

Hello

Mouthpiece

A telephone has two ends.
You say "Hello" into the end called the
mouthpiece.

The person you are phoning will hear the "Hello" in the end called the *earpiece*. The whole idea of the telephone is to get the "Hello" from your mouthpiece to the other person's earpiece.

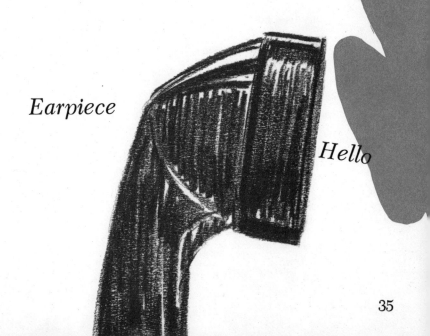

Earpiece

Hello

When you first say the "Hello," it has to go
through the air for a way.
So the "Hello" really starts as sound waves
in the air before it hits the mouthpiece.

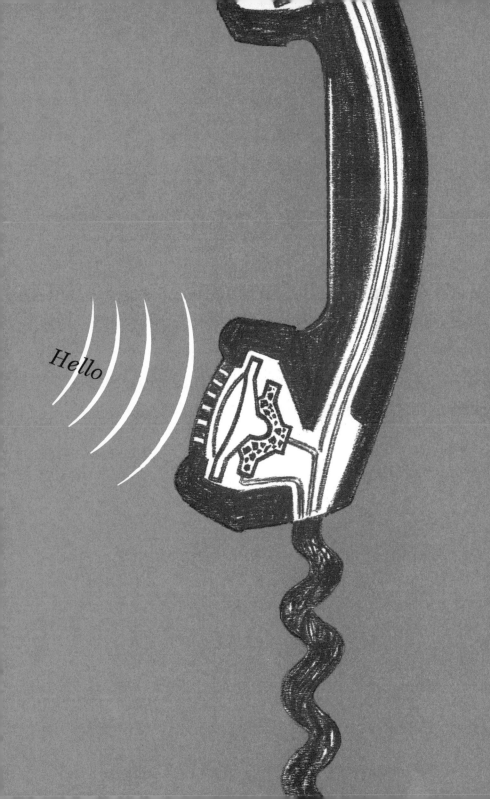

But when the "Hello" sound waves get inside
the mouthpiece something happens to
them.
They get changed into electrical pushes.
Scientists call these pushes *impulses*.

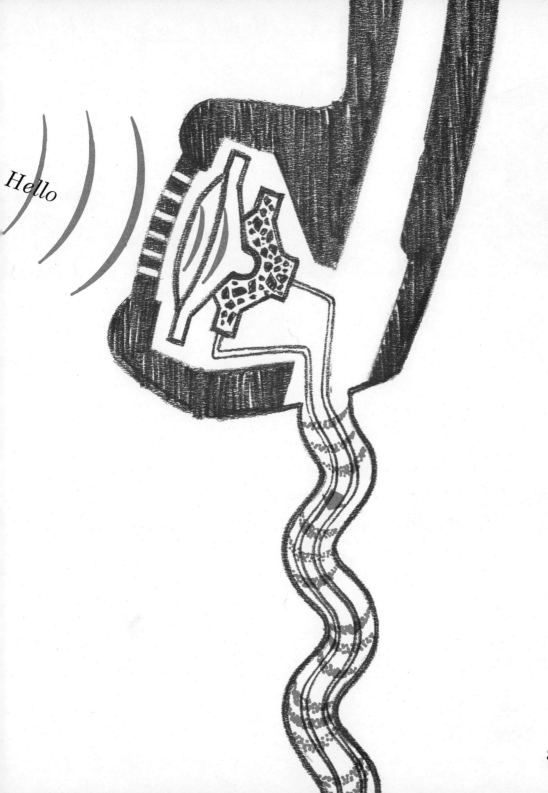

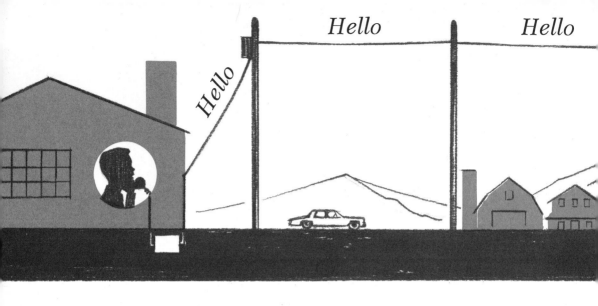

The impulses travel away from the
  mouthpiece along a wire.
The wire can stretch for a thousand miles
  or more.

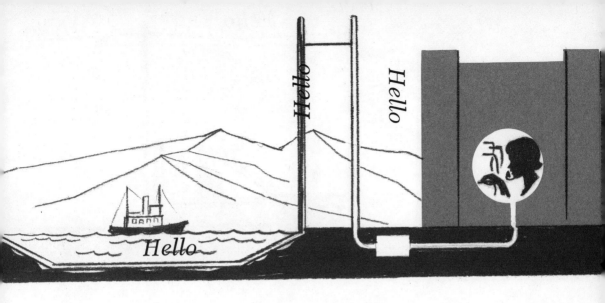

Usually you see it strung up on poles along
  roads.
But telephone wire can also be underground
  or underneath the water.

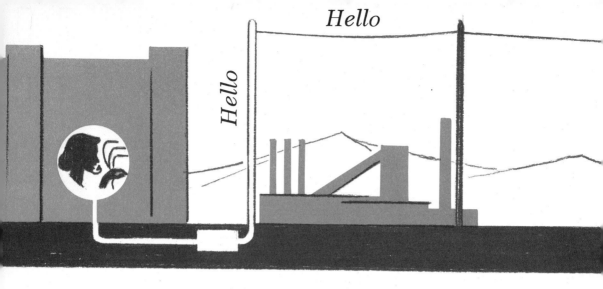

The impulses of the "Hello" travel so fast
they get to the person you are phoning
in just about no time at all.

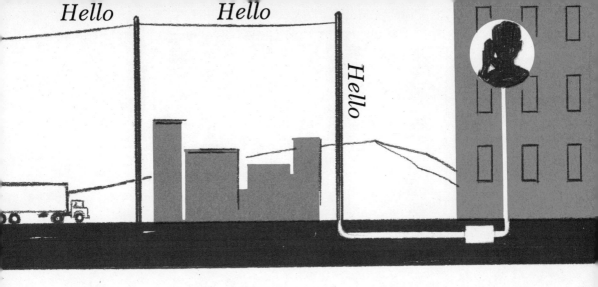

Hello *Hello* *Hello*

They get to the earpiece of the person you
are phoning.

The earpiece is the thing that changes the
   "Hello" impulses back into sound waves
   in the air.
Then the other person can hear the "Hello."
It will sound to him almost exactly like
   your voice.

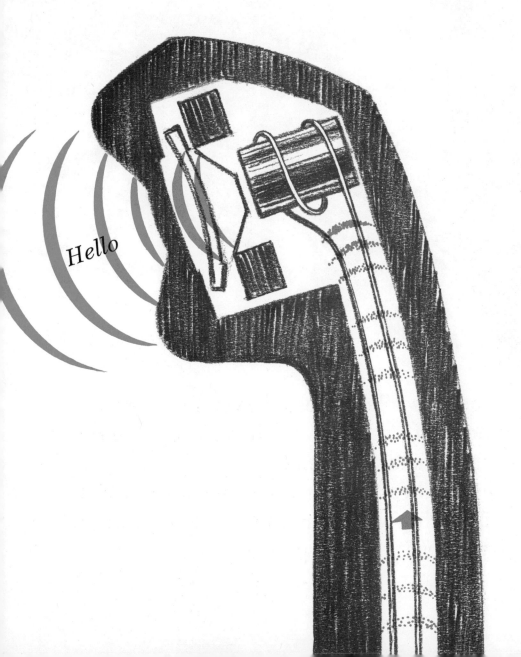

Hello

There are telephones all over the world.
When a lot of them are hooked up together,
  they make a *system*.
The world's telephone systems are hooked up
  in such a way that you can talk to anyone
  who can get to a phone.

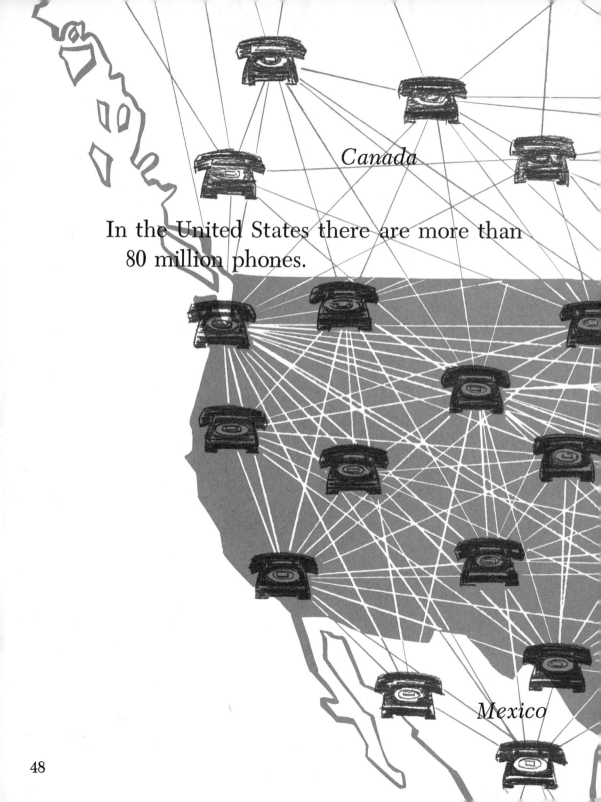

In the United States there are more than
80 million phones.

Canada

Mexico

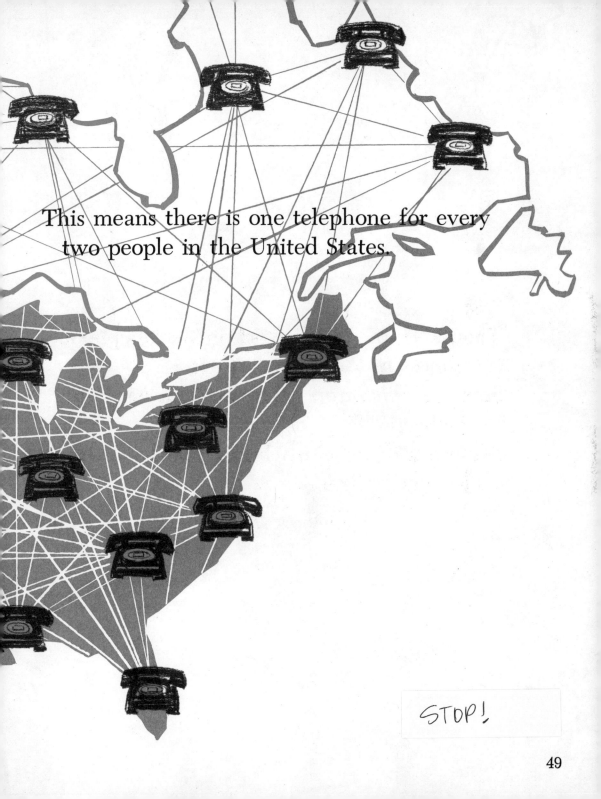

This means there is one telephone for every two people in the United States.

STOP!

Thousands of people work in the telephone
business in the United States.

Some are *operators* who help you get your
number.

Some are *repairmen* who fix phones when
they get broken.

Some are *linemen*
who look after the
millions of miles of
telephone wire.

Telephones have changed our lives in a lot
of ways.
They help us do business faster and better.
They help us find out whether people we
love are all right.
They save us time — all the time.
Phones are a big help to people.